THE COLORS OF LOVE

Love comes in many colors. With a little knowledge of love's rainbow you can mix and match the colors surrounding you to affect the love energy in your life:

Red for passion, courage, and strength

Pink for romance and tenderness

Puppy Love

A person's LOVE life may in-
volve more than people. If you
have pets, remember, they love
you too. To ENHANCE the love
and devotion of your dog or cat,
hang an amethyst from his or her
collar.

SECRET DESIRE SPELL

To win the HEART of the one you desire, write his or her name on an onion bulb during the waxing phase of the moon. Plant it in a brick-red pot filled with rich brown soil and water it daily while chanting your loved one's name. When the bulb roots, LOVE will take hold.

Love Spells

It was a common be-
lief in medieval times
that one of the most
powerful aphrodisi-
acs was a pinch of
ground unicorn horn
dissolved in a goblet
of red wine.

PURPLE RULES!

If you're planning a garden, think purple. Purple flowers are used in more LOVE SPELLS than any other color. The more purple flowers that you have on hand the better stocked your MAGIC "pantry" will be.

BECAUSE YOU NEVER KNOW

Next time you run your hands through his (or her) HAIR and accidentally pull out some loose STRANDS, save them! You never know how the relationship will unfold and those strands might be just what you need for a spell that calls for a lock of hair.

LIGHT a few candles. Sit back and relax. EXPERIMENT and have fun! You know what kind of love you want. Turn the page and find it.

Love Spells

lore to help steer love's energy your way. Consider it a starting point—advice on how to direct LOVE'S MAGIC—but in the end, you should let your instinct guide you. The best love spells are those you create yourself. Once you understand the psychological power of flowers, colors, symbols, and scents you can use them to influence your love life in exactly the manner you want.

life—it's called instinct. Your power tools? Love spells. ♥

LOVE SPELLS are prescriptions for empty beds, broken hearts, unfulfilled dreams. They offer ways to attract love, renew love, strengthen bonds, ignite passions, even silence gossip.

THIS BOOK is filled with love spells, potions, CHARMS, and

L o v e   S p e l l s

Introduction

Love is one of the few things in life you can never have too much of. Everyone loves and longs to be loved, and the more the better! TRUE LOVE, first love, romantic love, EROTIC LOVE, the love between friends, the love of one's self—there's no end to the variations. You already have the power to affect all sorts of love in your

5

Love Spells: *How to Work Your Mojo*
copyright © 2003 by Armand Eisen. All
rights reserved. Printed in China. No part
of this book may be used or reproduced in
any manner whatsoever without written
permission except in the case of reprints
in the context of reviews. For information
write Andrews McMeel Publishing, an
Andrews McMeel Universal company, 4520
Main Street, Kansas City, Missouri 64111.

Illustrations ©2003 by Lisa Parett

ISBN: 0-7407-3879-8
Library of Congress Catalog Card Number:
2003102684

LOVE SPELLS

HOW TO
WORK YOUR
Mojo

Debra Keller

Illustrated by Lisa Parett

Ariel Books

**Andrews McMeel
Publishing**

Kansas City

LOVE SPELLS

Yellow for healing and enlightenment

Green for new or growing love

Blue for patience and marriage

Violet for wisdom, communication, and physical love

Black for positivity

Inner Strength Spell

If you need help ending an unhealthy relationship, use your EYES. Rely on the darkening sky of a waning moon to strengthen your determination TO LET GO. Or go back in time to when you felt stronger by watching a CLOCK run BACKWARD in a mirror.

Love Spells

OLD-FASHIONED LOVE POTION

There's nothing like an old-fashioned love potion to fan the flames of DESIRE. Here's one to ignite your lover's passion:

$^1/_2$ cup water
$^1/_4$ cup red wine
A pinch of nutmeg
A bit of honey

Heat and serve warm.

EVERYONE
KNOWS . . .

Breaking a fruitcake
over the heads of a
new bride and groom
will bring them pros-
perity, eternal love,
good fortune, and
health.

FERTILITY SPELL

To increase your fertility, bring a sprig of fresh mistletoe into your home and let it dry completely. Then crush the dried leaves and store them in a yellow pouch tied with a violet ribbon. At night, slip the sachet under your pillow.

The Symbols of Love

Casting a LOVE SPELL has as much to do with your state of mind as it does with the INGREDIENTS you use. Before you cast your next spell, FORTIFY YOURSELF with an ancient SYMBOL of love. Use love's symbols to STRENGTHEN your resolve, increase your POSITIVE ENERGY, and make your LOVE MAGIC more powerful.

Love Spells

BELL, to attract the attentions of others

SWAN, to give birth to new love

STRING INSTRUMENTS, to hear your own heart's desires

ARROW, to send love's message
to someone else

OAK, to secure
eternal love

KNOT, for a faithful bond

Love Spells

KEY, to unlock the secrets of
another's heart

APPLE, the
symbol of true love

CLARITY SPELL

Love is wonderful but it can sometimes be CONFUSING. If you're unsure how you feel about someone try this clarity spell: To a small bowl of water, add three drops of rose oil, one rose petal, and an emerald-green stone. Wait three days, then remove the stone and hold it near your HEART. For better or worse,

in a short time your true feelings
will make themselves known, and
you will know what to do.

THE MYTHICAL MANDRAKE

The mandrake root is one of the earliest known APHRODISIACS (although we now know it's lethal). It's mentioned in ancient Greek and Roman texts, as well as in the Bible, but finding the MAGICAL ROOT isn't easy. According to ancient LORE, only mandrake roots grown under gal-

lows and pulled from the earth on a MOONLESS NIGHT by a string tied to a dog will do.

Love Be Eternally Young Spell

Yes, you can still have but-
terflies when you KISS, even
after you've been together for
years! To make an old love feel
exciting and new, leave a small
mirror where your lover will
find it. After the mirror has
reflected his or her image, break
it into small pieces. Bury the

pieces in a flower pot. Water
them daily to keep your LOVE
BLOOMING—and the butter-
flies in your stomach fluttering.

Black Magic

When it comes to love, BLACK is more than sexy—it's the color of a POSITIVE OUTLOOK. Surround yourself with black before a first date to increase the odds of a second one! Linger in a bathtub illuminated by BLACK CANDLES, wrap yourself in a black robe, then slip on a little black undergarment only you know is there.

Love Spells

READY FOR LOVE SPELL

When you're ready for new love to enter your life, eat three apricots. Dry the seeds, then store them in a small pink bag. Keep the bag near your bed—on a table, hanging from a bedpost, on top of a stack of bedside books—and be mindful of it as you fall asleep. Your dreams will awaken you to love's possibilities.

Come Hither, My Pet

One of history's most famous LOVE SPELLS was cast in the sixteenth century by Dr. John Fian of Scotland. Dr. Fian fell madly in love with the sister of one of his students. He asked the student to bring him three of his sister's hairs to use in a LOVE SPELL. Instead, the student brought the unsuspecting doctor three hairs

Love Spells

from a cow. But the spell worked!
For weeks afterward Dr. Fian was
followed around by his lovestruck
bovine companion.

EVERYONE KNOWS . . .

Love letters should always be written in ink and only mailed on Friday—that's the day associated with Venus, the ancient goddess of love.

SEXUALITY SPELL

Where there's smoke, there's fire . . . especially between the sheets. To IGNITE your lover's sexual passion, anoint a violet candle with a drop each of honey and rose oil. Light it and let it burn for three minutes. Immediately after blowing it out, pass a hair from your lover's head through its smoke. Repeat this rit-

ual at the same time for three con-
secutive nights. On the fourth
night, wrap the hair around the
candle, tie them together with
something red, and bury them near
an evergreen tree.

DON'T TRY THIS AT HOME

Albertus Magnus, the great medieval wizard, is considered by many to be the father of alchemy (the art of turning lead into gold), but he's also known for his romantic side. The legendary Magnus created a number of love potions. Here's one of his most potent concoctions:

Love Spells

200 ants
1 gallon of wine
200 wood lice
250 bees
Cinnamon

Mix the ants and wine in a glass jug, seal, and let stand for a month. Add the lice and let stand for another month. Add the bees and let stand for a third month. Add cinnamon to taste and serve.

EVERYONE
KNOWS . . .

Bananas are the fruit of male fertility, but not because of their phallic shape. Eating three bananas at a time is said to increase a man's sperm count.

Don't Let It End Spell

To regain the attentions of a lover you feel slipping away, place two red candles side by side, but six inches apart. Tie one end of a black ribbon around each candle. Every morning give the ribbon a slight pull—as you do, the candles should be drawn together, and your partner's attentions be redrawn to you.

THE LANGUAGE OF FLOWERS

Flowers speak the LANGUAGE OF LOVE. In Victorian times they were used to convey secret messages of the heart—to communicate what society tried to silence. Today the language of flowers is still in BLOOM . . . if you know how to speak it.

Love Spells

APPLE BLOSSOM: I think you are beautiful.

♥

BELLFLOWER: Meet me in the morning.

CHERRY BLOSSOM: I hope our friendship blossoms into something more.

EVENING PRIMROSE: I adore you.

FOXGLOVE: You are too shallow for me.

GLADIOLUS: I'm upset by what you said.

HONEYSUCKLE: Please marry me.

JONQUIL: Please tell me how you feel.

Love Spells

LOOSESTRIFE: I'm sorry.

MISTLETOE: A thousand kisses.

PASSIONFLOWER: My heart belongs to someone else.

SNOWDROP: Can we try again?

TRUMPET FLOWER: I want you passionately.

Gossip Ending Spell

Loose lips sink ships . . . and sometimes love affairs. To protect your relationship from the evils of gossip, make this simple charm. You'll need the following:

12 inches of yellow ribbon
1 small orange or tangerine
9 straight pins

Love Spells

Whole cloves

Powdered orris root

1 violet-scented candle or 1 stick
   of incense

Tie the ribbon around the orange
and secure it with the straight
pins. Knot the top of the ribbon to
make a loop. Prick the orange
peel with the tip of a knife and
into each cut insert a clove. Do
this as many times as you desire.

Roll the orange in the orris root. Light the candle or incense. Then pass your charm though the scented smoke three times while incanting:

May this charm of orris and cloves
Silence gossip and help love grow.

If an unmarried girl
wants a new boyfriend,
she should sweep all
the cobwebs from her
home.

Love at First Sight Charm

Love at first sight can be both exhilarating and torturous. What if the two of you don't see each other again? Here's a charm to ensure you do:

Pick two long and pliable rosemary stems and tie them together in the shape of a heart. Wrap the

heart with green ribbon while re-
peating this spell:

FATE BROUGHT US TOGETHER
    AND WON'T KEEP US
    APART.

AS ROSEMARY DRIES, OUR
    NEW LOVE WILL START.

Love Stones and Metals

Gemstones and metals have been used to manipulate love for centuries. They've been meditated upon, touched, carried, given, and worn. With a little understanding of how they work, you can use them to influence your love life. Use:

Love Spells

SILVER, to enhance understanding and illuminate love from
within.

COPPER, to attract romance and
increase sexuality.

AMETHYST, to fortify existing
love.

CORAL, to attract new love.

ROSE QUARTZ, to heals love's wounds.

EMERALDS, to ensure honesty.

JADE, to enhance inner beauty and attract erotic love.

LAPIS LAZULI, to strengthen spiritual love.

Love Spells

LODESTONE, to strengthen the power of any love spell.

MALACHITE, to deepen one's ability to love.

MOONSTONE, to attract passionate love.

SAPPHIRE, to ensure fidelity and strengthen commitment.

WISHBONE MAGIC

Breaking a WISHBONE is fine for most wishes, but not when it comes to love. If your wish is for a new lover, don't let that bone break! Instead, hold it in your left hand while ENVISIONING the partner of your dreams. Then, NAIL THE BONE over your front door to invite him or her into your life.

THE POETRY OF LOVE

Those INTIMATE with William Butler Yeats know he created more than poetry—he also created love potions. His best-known potion is said to be INFALLIBLE: the powdered liver of a black cat steeped in tea and poured from a black teapot.

Love Spells

On Valentine's night,
if you want to dream
of a future lover, sleep
with two laurel leaves
under your pillow.

Passion on the Streets

Ancient Romans knew where to find LOVE—on the streets! (No, it's not what you think!) Lovelorn Romans could buy ready-made LOVE POTIONS from kindly old ladies who sold their wares on the street. Their INGREDIENTS were less than appealing: pigeon blood, hairs from wolves' tails, colts' scalps, granulated snake

skeletons, and the powdered bones of toads whose carcasses had been picked clean by ants, TO NAME A FEW.

Attraction Spell

To attract the ATTENTION of someone you long for, dab three drops of rose oil on a ginseng root. LIGHT A RED CANDLE, then pass the root through its smoke thirteen times while RECITING your desired's name. Bury the root where he will pass it daily (even a planter box outside his workplace will do).

Love Spells

Each time he walks by the buried ginseng root he'll THINK OF YOU.

Love Is in the Air

Sometimes love really *is* in the air. PERFUMED OILS have been used since ancient times to attract, ENCHANT, or keep lovers. A few drops of oil added to a bath, a stick of incense, or a SCENTED CANDLE can all have IRRESISTIBLE powers.

To ATTRACT PURE LOVE, use

Love Spells

honeysuckle, jasmine, lavender, or rose.

To arouse sexual desire, use musk, vanilla, or violet.

To ensure fidelity, use magnolia.

To attract a spouse, use apple or orange blossoms.

Peace Spell

To quiet an argument and heal a misunderstanding try a dab of PEACE OIL:

1 ounce sunflower oil
6 drops rose oil
6 drops lavender oil

Dip the tip of your finger in the oil, then GENTLY TOUCH your

Love Spells

lover. You'll open the path of communication while your physical
connection will RECONNECT
your hearts.

CHOCOLATE SPELL

Modern scientists have discovered what CASANOVAS have known for centuries—that a chemical in chocolate arouses feelings of love (DUH!). But what they don't know yet is that CHOCOLATE CHARGED with this simple love spell can be even more potent:

Love Spells

MAY THESE CHOCOLATES
DARK AND SWEET
FILL YOUR HEART WITH
DESIRE FOR ME.

Cinnamon and Spice and Everything Nice

According to ancient love lore, cinnamon is bursting with male SEXUALITY, and nutmeg is decidedly female. For a night of intense lovemaking, try mixing the two spices in equal amounts, then dissolve them in a mug of hot chocolate—for the two of you to share, of course.

Love Spells

EVERYONE
KNOWS . . .

If your shoelaces come
undone, a future lover
is thinking about you.

Moon Magic

Before you cast a love spell, be
sure to LOOK AT THE MOON—
it's a celestial guide to the energy
of love. Spells that banish people
or unwelcome feelings should
be cast during the MOON'S
WANING phase. The waxing phase
is best for spells that attract or
FORTIFY LOVE. A full moon
makes any spell all the more

POWERFUL, and a moonless sky means you should take the night off!

Oops, I Changed My Mind Spell

You discover Mr. or Ms. Right is actually Mr. or Ms. Wrong. How do you get out of it gracefully? With tender communication of course, but a little love magic can't hurt. On a white piece of paper, write that person's name, followed by the words *No More*. Then core an apple,

tuck the paper inside, and bury it.
As the apple withers, so will his
or her interest in you.

Come Back Spell

To hasten the return of an absent lover, pluck the first flower you see in May. Blow gently on the petals, then say:

FLOWER PINK, FLOWER BLUE
I WISH TO SEE MY LOVER TRUE.

Your lover will come, although it may not be who you expect!

Love Spells

RED-HOT LOVE

Red is the color of PASSIONATE love. If you find something red, keep it! A piece of ribbon, a thread, or a flower petal could be an omen of love's dramatic entrance. Keep your eyes and ears open and your HEART READY.

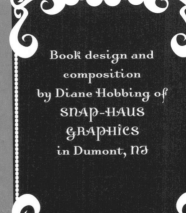

Book design and
composition
by Diane Hobbing of
SNAP-HAUS
GRAPHICS
in Dumont, NJ